God Moments

Recognizing God's Presence in the ordinary

Sister Kathleen M. O'Connell, RSM

For the Beauty of the Earth

1. For the beauty of the earth, for the glory of the skies,
for the love which from our birth over and around us lies.
Refrain:
Lord of all, to you we raise
this, our hymn of grateful praise.

2. For the wonder of each hour of the day and of the night,
hill and vale and tree and flower, sun and moon and stars of light, [Refrain]

3. For the joy of ear and eye, for the heart and mind's delight,
For the mystic harmony linking sense to sound and sight:

4. For the joy of human love, brother, sister, parent, child,
friends on earth, and friends above, for all gentle thoughts and mild, [Refrain]

5 For yourself, best gift divine, to the world so freely given,
agent of God's grand design: peace on earth and joy in heaven. [Refrain]

Folliott Sandford Pierpoint, 1835-1917

Introduction

In 2018, when I began writing these reflections, coupling them with my photographs and sending them into cyberspace, I never expected that they would be compiled into a book. I am humbled by the reaction "the Footprints of God" has engendered. Now I have gathered my reflections into a second book. "God Moments" continues what was started in the first book, namely that our lives are filled with instances during which our Loving Creator God has made his presence known to us. The ordinary moments become extra-ordinary. Many of these reflections were written as we were isolated during the years of Covid 19, hard days for many people.

A "God Moment" is when our senses are awakened to the presence of God in the people, events, and challenges of daily living. It is in these very ordinary experiences of our daily living that we will find God. Often, it is in retrospect that we realize how a loving God has made himself known to us. We are led to give praise and gratitude for his goodness, and challenged to follow his Way. I pray that these reflections will enable you to see how God has been present to you as you go through each day, in the good as well as in the difficult moments. Know that in those moments you are being blessed by God.

One of the critical concerns of the Sisters of Mercy is the care for our earthly home, for its sustainability and vitality. We are called to be faithful stewards of all that has been entrusted to us. My reflections continue to recognize the beauty that is all around us. Our Creator God has blessed us with so much. While we often feel there is not much we can do on a global scale to effect environmental change such as climate, water resources, extractivism, etc., it is in the little things we do each day that will protect our environment and preserve our planet for future generations.

This book is not intended to be read in one sitting. Instead, each reflection offers the possibility of recalling when you have been touched by the presence of our God. May it lead you to discover or rediscover you own "God Moments."

In Appreciation

I am continually grateful to a loving God who has blessed me with the gift of seeing the beauty of his creation and of being able to capture that beauty through the lens of a camera. He continues to bless me with the ability to use words to celebrate that beauty, I have been blessed!

I am grateful to all those who have encouraged me to continue to share my photos and reflections, whether through the book "Footprints of God", or via the wonders of the internet. You have gifted me with your kind words and have shared stories of how a reflection may have helped or encouraged you. I have been blessed by all of you.

The challenge of writing a book is followed by the challenge of correct spelling and grammar. Spellcheck doesn't always work and the grammar police don't always catch all the typos. I am grateful for the proof-readers who checked for spelling and punctuation: Sister Veronica Casey, RSM, who taught me to type at Mercy High School those many years ago, and Sister Diane Marie Erskine, RSM, who has admitted to being one of those spelling and grammar police. A thank you also, to Patty and Frank Cost for their assistance in formatting this book. Any typos and mistakes are my fault.

I am grateful to my family, especially my Mom and Dad, Isabelle and Florence O'Connell who instilled in me a love of God and a love for God's creation. I thank my religious family, the Sisters of Mercy, who have encouraged the writing of this book and whose concern for Mother Earth has provided inspiration for my reflections.

I am dedicating this book to the new generations of my O'Connell clan, and to the new generations of **all** our families, in whose hands rest the future of our earth. May their days be filled with "God Moments" and may they accept the challenge of being worthy stewards of God's creation. I love and pray for each and everyone of you.

Peace be with you, my friend!

"Let us hold unswervingly to the hope we profess, for he who promised is faithful."

Hebrews 10:23

A Reason to Hope! The snow covered crocuses bravely pop their heads out of the frozen ground and give us a reason to hope. Nurtured in the cold, dark winter bosom of Mother Earth, they are one of the first harbingers of spring. Their bright colors of purples, yellows and whites gleefully announce to us that we have made it through another winter. Surely there remain more cold and snow in our forecasts, but we know that it will be short lived. The crocus give us reason to hope. A hope that, though we go through dark days when our spirits seem low, we can find around us signs of new life, of promise, of future. Sometimes they may be hidden under a cover of snow. We, too, are signs of Hope. Our hope is in the Lord who is with us always. Look for signs of his presence. Be his sign of hope for others. Happy Hope-filled Spring!

Spring - Garden early bloomers.

"Come and see the works of God, awesome in the deeds done for us."

Ps. 66:5

Each year, the George Eastman House in Rochester, NY celebrates Mr. Eastman's passion for bulb flowers with a glorious display of all varieties and colors of tulips, daffodils, iris, hyacinths, and more – all grown from little bulbs. This display is usually held mid-winter, February, when we all need to see the promise of spring. These little bulbs, some as small as your thumb, are covered with dried up layers of tissue-thin skin that protect the inner core. To the non-gardener, one wonders how something that ugly can become something so beautiful. Yet the gardener knows that at the core lies the promise of something great. With care and nurturing, that ugly little bulb transforms into a flower of amazing complexity. So it is with people. Sometimes all we see are the dried-up exteriors and we are ready to ignore the person. Yet, each person has an inner core that holds something beautiful. There is promise there to be discovered. Let us be patient gardeners to each other, caring for and nurturing the goodness in one another. Let us allow the Master Gardener to work his miracle in us and each other. We are creations of promise and beauty.

Spring Bulb Display George Eastman House, Rochester, NY

Weaving threads to make cloth is one of those amazing inventions of Ancient Peoples. The basics of weaving remain to this day. Vertical threads, the "warp", will determine the length and width of the cloth. In a sense, they provide the stability of the fabric. The "weft" are the horizontal threads that are woven in and out the warp creating the color, texture and pattern. Our lives might be likened to the weaving process. Our "warp" consists of those values we hold: such as family, faith, virtues, the principles we live by. They give us the stability upon which we weave our fabric. The "weft" are the threads of our daily lives woven in and out of the "warp" and showing the different colors and textures present in our lives. Perhaps the bright colors of surprises, happy moments long forgotten, gentle colors of the moments of peace, subdued colors of grief, sadness, pain. Our "weft" varies as we weave our way through life. There may be some knots and loose ends because we are always adding new textures and colors. But all are blended together with the "warp" of our values creating a tapestry uniquely our own. We are a work in progress.

Weavers' Studio

"She obtains wool and flax and makes cloth with skillful hands."

Proverbs 31:13

May all the peoples praise you."

Ps. 67:4

I have to admit it. I am addicted to jigsaw puzzles. When I see one started, I just have to stop and try to fit in a piece. Or two or ten. The most frustrating thing for a "puzzler" is to have finished a puzzle only to find there is a piece missing. And the search is on. Everyplace is a possible hiding place. Vacuum cleaner bags have been know to have been emptied in the search. There is no rest until the missing piece has been found. Then we can call the puzzle "complete."

Think of community like a puzzle made up of all different people. It can be a family, a workplace, our faith community. There is a place for each one of us. We are incomplete if there is someone estranged from the community. It may be because of a difference in opinion, lifestyle, a feeling of not being wanted, a sense of inadequacy. Even illness keeps us shut off from the others. Unfortunately, there are many empty spots in our communities these days. Are we as enthusiastic about finding, inviting, reconciling, and welcoming that missing person as we would the missing puzzle piece?

Puzzle time

"Trust in God's faithful love forever."

Ps 52:10.

The walk with my three year old great niece over an old lift bridge went well until we got to the middle. Suddenly my niece just froze in place. Being able to look through the holes of the steel mesh that made up the roadway and to see the water below was a bit too much for her feelings of safety. The fact that the bridge seemed to shake each time a car passed by didn't help much either. So I picked her up and continued to cross. Gradually I could sense her body relaxing as I carried her along. She wasn't alone.

In these days of uncertainty, we are all feeling caught on the bridge. Sometimes we get frozen in our tracks as it all seems to be too much. We begin to imagine all kinds of bad things are going to happen. We are frightened and we panic. But we need to know that there is Someone walking that bridge with us, carrying us along if need be; Someone who can relieve our anxiety, who can show us the way across, who has promised to be with us. Trust in the Lord. Even a weak, muffled cry of "help" will do it. And know that the Lord will carry you through.

Golden Gate Bridge, San Francisco, CA

"Lord,

teach me

delight

in simple things."

Anon.

A moment in time! How often do we look at our watches and wonder where the time went. Sometimes we don't even remember the small details of our day. Certainly there are the mundane tasks we casually do over and over. But there are moments that cause us to step aside and become aware of who we are, where we are, and what we are about. But unless we become mindful of the moment, it is gone, forgotten, and we wonder where the time went. These little moments can be God-moments, times when we become aware of God's action in our lives. It can be a moment of beauty, an encounter with another, the accomplishment of a task, or just a quiet pause in the rush in our lives. It may be suffering a slight, making a mistake, forgetting an appointment. Perhaps taking a bit of time each night before sleep to look back at these moments will help us become more mindful of God's presence through, with, and in us. And soon we will be more mindful of where the time went.

Jensen Beach, FL

> "May God ... encourage your hearts and strengthen them."
>
> 2 Thess 2:17

Certainly, this is a "sign of the times". It is found woven through the mesh of the fence. At the end of the fence are the words "Alsan to Lucy". I can only imagine the story behind this. Perhaps words of encouragement to someone who is sick, or frightened, or lonely. Or perhaps just an expression of love and hope to a loved one in this time of worry and discouragement. "Lucy" is each of us. It is a reminder to each of us that we need to call upon our reserves of courage as we face the difficulties of each day. It is courage that causes us to seek ways to keep in touch with each other; to live a simpler lifestyle when we are accustomed to having more; to risk ways that help others in need while facing diminished paychecks or none at all. Courage is one of the gifts of the Holy Spirit that we received at our confirmation. We need to pray that the Spirit will send courage upon us when we feel discouraged, worn down, fearful. Courage doesn't travel alone. It will bring with it the virtue of Hope: a hope that things will work out for the better, that we will be safe and comforted, that the Lord is with us on this journey. "Courage, dear heart"!

"Courage, Dear Heart" - sign on fence, Wisconsin St., Rochester, NY

Last summer, the hydrangea bush outside my front door only had about 5 blooms. Pink blooms. It was very disappointing. This summer, the bush must have realized that we needed cheering up and it is giving out dozens of blooms. To my surprise, the pink bush has turned into a glorious multi-colored display of pinks, blues, lavenders. This particular bloom seems to be a unique blend of all the colors at once. Each of the colors has its say in the beauty that is the result of their coming together. We can learn much from this little bush. As each bloom revels in the gift of its color, so each of us enjoy our own gifts and talents that make us uniquely individual. But it is when we join together our individual gifts that we create something new and beautiful. It will be an entity that reflects the beauty of each of us and displays the goodness of all of us. The Master Gardener is at work among us. Do we let him till the soil and water us? Do we see that when we put aside our prejudices and blend our gifts and talents, we are a part of a new creation? How can you blend your gifts and talents with someone else's that results in a new creation? "Behold I make all things new." Rev 21:5

"Each flower, in its uniqueness, blesses the garden."

Anon

Convent flowers, St. James, Whittington Rd. Rochester. NY

"We will be known forever by the tracks we leave."

Native American Proverb

It snowed yesterday. We haven't had much snow this year so it was still a welcome sight. As I stood inside watching the fluffy white stuff fall from the sky covering the dried grasses and left-over leaves, I marveled at its pristine beauty. The yard was like a newly crafted canvas with no footprints marring its surface. And it was quiet. It wouldn't be long before the squirrels and rabbits come hopping through. And the little dogs and big dogs that roam the neighborhood. But for now the snow covered yard before me was full of possibilities. It was like the new day I was beginning. A new start. Each day begins with a clean slate. What kind of tracks will I leave behind as I set out on my day? Will they be helter-skelter with no direction? With no discernible plan? I don't know exactly what will be before me this day but if I wear the shoes of kindness, generosity and love, people will see my tracks and recognize that God has walked this way. I pray that this will be so. What tracks will you leave behind this day? Know that your footsteps can bring Christ's Mercy and love to others. And if the spirit moves you. Go build a snowperson! "This is the Day the Lord has made. Let us rejoice and be glad!"

Durand Eastman Park, Rochester, NY

We're expecting! News indeed! Rather, the robins who have built their nest on our back porch are expecting. Four little blue eggs waiting to be incubated and hatched. Soon Mom and Pop Robin will be searching the grass for bits of morsels to feed their little ones. Do they know that what they are expecting will change their lifestyle by the very nature of what they are created to be?

What does it mean to "be expecting"? "Expecting" means to be anticipating what is to come to be. Sometimes we know what we are expecting: a gift desired, an action anticipated, a result of some encounter with another. But there are the hidden expectations that we don't even realize we have. And expectations that are unwanted. We use the expression "waiting for the other shoe to drop" for those unwanted, negative outcomes. Sometimes that can be a self-fulfilling prophecy. But what if we started our day expecting that good things will occur, expecting that God will be present in the moments of our day, that His Presence will help us deal with the unexpected. What if each night we took the time to remember and thank God for those unexpected moments when our hearts were touched by goodness, knowing that there is good in each moment. So what if the other shoe falls, at least now you have a pair of shoes. And there is good to be found in that.

"Waiting patiently in expectation."

H. Nouwan

Spring robin's nest, back porch

"In my God is the joy of my soul."

Isaiah 61:10

June's flower is the Rose. The garden nursery named this rose "Love and Peace". It is now the newest member of my garden and has already blessed me with its first bloom. It truly lives up to its name. Looking at it, healthy and strong, the rose does indeed speak of love and peace. Love, the yellow, comes from the center and, as it gently spreads its petals out, it brings with it a beautiful tinge of pink: Peace. Its gentle fragrance fills the heart and quiets the mind.

True Love comes from our deepest center where we find the love of God. A healthy and strong Love cannot help but spill out around us, changing the color of our surroundings with varying shades of Peace. This rose is a reminder of who I am called to be - a person of Love and Peace. I pray that my fragrance, and yours, will be the bearer of Love and Peace to those we encounter in our day to day living. We know how to do it. Just do it!

Garden Rose, Rochester, NY

"Be still and know that I am God." Ps. 46:10

Come into the garden and rest awhile. The stillness of the garden soothes my noisy, busy heart. Slowly the human-made sounds drift away and nature's sounds fill the quiet. The steady buzzing of the bee as it moves from flower to flower. The rustle of the leaves dancing in the breezes. And up in the branches comes the too, too, too of the cardinal as it calls out to its mate. A far away echo repeats the message. Spots of color flit by – a yellow finch, a blue jay, the red cardinal. Daisies and cosmos nod and bob to the sounds of nature's music. Don't watch your clock. There is no time in a garden. Just be! Dorothy Frances Gurney says it well in her poem, God's Garden:

One is nearer God's heart in a garden

Garden, Winton Rd., Rochester, NY

The day lilies have had their say in the garden and now it is time for the Hydrangeas to show off their splendor. The bushes by the front door have outdone themselves this summer. Pinks, lavenders, blues – all blending into large globes of color. It is as if they knew we needed a big splash of color to offset the dark days of covid 19's winter. This particular hydrangea is a type called "Lace Cap" hydrangea. It has been more visible in home gardens the last few years. More flat than round, it has a crown of single blossoms surrounding a circle of very tiny little buds that open up into tiny star shaped blooms. But don't be misled by its delicate appearance. It is a hardy plant with strong stems and large green leaves. And it does what God has created it to do. It shows off the beauty of a God who has filled us with awe and wonder at his creation. We have been blessed by yet another footprint of God.

"At the work of your hands I shout for joy."

Ps. 92:5

Summer in the convent garden at St. James

"Proclaim with joy, the harmony and beauty of all creation."

Ps. 98:1

I heard the sweetest, gentlest sound among the trees in The Boston Commons. It didn't take long to identify where the music originated. Away from the noise of the congested streets, the music calmed my spirit and made me want to just sit and soak it all in. This instrument of such peace-inducing sounds was new to me. Was it Asian in origin? I surmised this because the artist playing it was obviously Asian. No matter. The music coming forth from such a simple looking object was enough. As I stood and listened to his playing, I was amazed how little attention people paid to his music. They hurried by on the paths of the Commons not hearing the gift of peace he was offering them. Too turned into their air buds and phones, they didn't know what they were missing. And I wondered, too, how much music I have failed to hear because I have been too preoccupied by the other noises around me. I am grateful to this gentleman for the gift he gave me for a few short moments. And I pray that I may not only stop to "smell the daisies" but to also quiet myself to hear the "sounds of music" they make. May our ears be opened to welcome the music of God's creation, God's world. Easy listening, indeed!

Boston Commons - Erhu, a Chinese musical string instrument

"Every moment of the year has its own beauty."

RW Emerson

Now is the time of the year when we see colorful displays of the earth's bounty. I saw this strange looking squash in a nursery garden display in Haverhill, MA last week. It is called a "peanut squash". That is because, as the squash grows, peanut shell-like protrusions appear on the outside of the squash. The sugars in the flesh begin leeching through the skin and cause these unique wart-like bumps. The more they grow, the sweeter the squash becomes. I have never eaten one but they say that the flesh is very delicious and has a smooth texture. Its appearance is a little off-setting but the inside is good. A bit like us humans. Sometimes we are a bit covered by the warts of our human frailties. But when we take the time to look behind the warts, we will most often find the goodness with which God has blessed us. So, let's not be put off by what seems different to us. We all have "warts" that hide our inner spirit. Take time to find the sweetness in yourself and in one another. Remember that the Master Gardener has found us worthy to be included in the bounty of the harvest.

Fall: - Peanut Squash, Farmers Marken, Haverhill, MA

"How glorious your dwelling place, O Lord of hosts."

Ps. 84:1

Once again, God's creation on display! The power and the beauty of the crashing surf leaves one awestruck at this force of nature. Twice daily the incoming tide rushes along the rocky jetty giving one pause to marvel at the magnificent picture it leaves on the mind. Truthfully, it is sometimes easier to see God's hand in the majesty of the surf than is to see God's hand in the grains of sand on the beach, grains worked over by the action of the tide and boulders for millions of years. Yet God's hand is no less present in the grain of sand on the beach. God works in our lives in the same way. There are certainly moments when we are overwhelmed by the creative energy of a loving God. And these are wonderful moments to treasure. But God is just as present in the day to day grains of life that surround us. Perhaps not as profoundly but certainly every bit as real. And those who have eyes to see.... What do you see?

Summer - Jetty at Hampton Beach State Park, MA

Sometimes it can happen overnight, sometimes the transformation will take days. These leaves are on their way to full color but it will take some time yet. Nature tells us that change takes time. Change is inevitable. We cannot avoid it, it happens for better or for worse. We age, we mature, we grow old. It can't be hurried and can't be stopped but it is always coming. There are times when we might resist change and there are definitely times when the changes that occur are not good for the human spirit. Like the leaves, we are God's signs of change. We realize that our society is hurting right now. Divisions and hatred seem to be more and more prevalent. Remembering that the Word of God can effect a more powerful change, we need to turn to God's Word to learn how to go about being that instrument of change. Perhaps we feel what we do is insignificant in the large scheme of things, but how you live today and tomorrow brings a change in the world that you call home. St. Francis prays that we may be an instrument of Peace. We pray that we may be that and also instruments of good change to bring love and justice to a hurting world. Be the change you want to see.

Fall leaves, Rochester, NY

"Be the change you want to see."

Anon

"Our hearts can always be in the same place, centered in God."

C. McAuley

My friend's husband recently died and she was sharing with me some of the things she missed doing with him. "They are all wonderful memories," she said, "but what I miss the most is our praying together before settling into sleep". This was their every night blessing for each other, the time when they shared their love for God in prayer. I recall, when I was a child of about six, bursting into my parents' bedroom (yes, I was supposed to be asleep) and hearing them pray with each other. It stopped me short at the door and I quietly moved away because even at that age I recognized something special was happening. What a wonderful gift it is for a child to hear his/her parents praying. Do couples do this anymore? I think of the possibilities that come from this practice. I think of the peace that comes into one's heart when sharing one's love of God with another person who loves that same God. I think of the forgiveness that has to happen when both are coming together before the Lord. I see the hope that springs forth when one is sharing what God has placed in one's heart. I see a love that grows deeper because its source comes from the Lord.

Summer sunset, Webster, NY

> *"A day hemmed in prayer is less likely to unravel."*
>
> Anon

Is it ever too late to start praying with another? It may be a spouse, a close friend, a mentor. Perhaps it might feel embarrassing to pray out loud but time will take care of that. What to pray? How to pray? Maybe begin with the Lord's prayer, saying it together. And then asking for help in the needs of the day, in the family. Be faithful to just that simple start and the Lord will lead you to more. Give it time, don't neglect it. And what does one do when the one with whom you shared prayer is no longer there? Keep praying, knowing that the beloved one is still praying with you in your heart. You will know their prayer is there. Perhaps it might be helpful to think of a close friend and invite them into your mind and heart to pray with you. Ask the Lord to be with this person at this time and to send his blessings upon him/her. Pray for your soul-friend and with him/her.

Summer ocean view, Maine

"Flowers always make people better, happier, and more helpful; they are sunshine, food and medicine for the soul."

(Luther Burbank)

Isn't that the truth! Isn't that why we send people flowers when they are going through a bad time? It is our way of hoping to heal the weary heart. And our way of celebrating that which is good and positive in our lives. Flowers by their very nature give us hope. Look what they have become since being first planted in the garden. In those tiny seeds reside the potential for great beauty and joy. What was once dry and hard has bloomed into something wonderful. Summer is a glorious reminder of possibility and hope. With all that color and vibrancy we can't help but feel our hearts lift. God's love comes to us in tones of pinks, blues, yellows, reds, certainly green (must be God's favorite color because there is so much of it). Let the magic of flowers fill you. Find a flowered place and sit in it for awhile. Soak in the beauty. Soak up the sunshine, food and medicine they offer. You will feel better, and your day will seem fuller. Don't forget to share some flowers with friends so they, too, can feel the magic and wonder God has created for us.

Summer daisies

"Give thanks to the Lord, for He is good."

Ps 136:1

Preceded by hundreds of other marchers and dozens of floats and balloons, these stalwart marchers managed to keep our attention because of the precision with which they marched. Marching bands don't just happen. They come as the result of hours of practice and drilling. Our celebration of giving thanks also does not come about overnight. A heart full of gratitude isn't just a Thanksgiving thing. It is an attitude that is obtained only by much thought and practice. It calls us to be constantly aware of the goodness of a Loving God who blesses us with so many riches. Notice how the poorest among us seem to know how to give thanks to the One who is Creator. Perhaps they know even better because they are grateful for even the little they have. And we, who have much, often take that "much" for granted and forget to give praise and thanks where it is due. To have "an attitude of gratitude" we need to daily give thanks to our God, to practice being aware that all in our day is gift, every day! Count your blessings daily, give praise and thanks to the one who has blessed us. Let Thanksgiving Day this year be a summation of all the blessings of the year.

Macy's Thanksgiving Day Parade, New York, NY

When the signers of the Declaration of Independence 246 years ago put their names on this monumental document, they no doubt recognized the long task that lay ahead in the formation of a new government. The Constitution might never had been ratified if the framers hadn't promised to add a Bill of Rights. The first ten amendments to the Constitution gave citizens more confidence in the new government and contain many of today's American's most valued freedoms. What we often fail to recognize is the fact that these freedoms aren't just for individuals alone but are established for the common good of all. Much of the tension we feel today is often caused by what people feel is a violation of MY rights. The Common Good takes a back seat while individuals put their own interests over the basic human rights of all. With the freedoms we have been given comes the responsibility to see that all enjoy them equally. We say in our pledge to the flag of the United States "one nation, under God, with liberty and justice for all." Do we try to live this pledge? Do we do what we can to ensure that basic human needs from conception to death are met? We have the responsibility to see that all share in these same freedoms given to us. There is still much work to be done.

Flag display on porch in East Aurora,

"One nation, under God, indivisible, with Liberty and Justice for all."

Pledge of Allegiance

This year, my first visit to Highland Park happened earlier than usual and I found a sight that I hadn't realized takes place each year. All through the park was a ground covering of blue and white tiny flowers, creating a carpet spread out under the still unleafed trees. The more I walked into the park, the more splendid did the carpet become. Individually, the tiny little star shaped blossoms stood strong in the hard, dried winter dirt. Collectively, they displayed a strong visual of what could be when all came together. A blue carpet of promise causing me to reflect on what possibilities there can be when we all come together. Because of concern over the Covid 19 virus the last three years, we have had to stand alone at times. We have tried to be stalwart in the face of the issues resulting from the virus: health, economy, loneliness, stress, isolation, etc.. But we have stood strong! We have now come to an end of the emergency restrictions. It is time to stand together once again, to remember what we can collectively do when we come together. This Easter season reminds us of the newness of life given to us by the Creator of all life. As the people of God we can work together to overcome the injustices and inequalities of this time. The carpet of blue shows that we collectively have the power to create great beauty in this earth we call home.

"Nature does not hurry, yet everything is accomplished."
Lan Tao

Early Spring, Highland Park, Rochester, NY

"You will never wash my feet!"

John 13:8

We know the story. Jesus gathered with his disciples to share the Passover meal. As he prepares to do the ritual of the washing of the feet of the guests, good old Peter resists having Jesus minister to him. "Not I, Lord," he protests. The Lord tells Peter that if he wants to be a part of him, he must let him wash his feet. He tells the disciples, and us, that he has given us a model to follow. We should do likewise. But let's reverse the picture and see ourselves on the recipient side of the coin, Peter's side. How do we react to the gestures of others to do things for us? Since the age of two, we have insisted on an "I can do it myself!" attitude. We are uncomfortable when someone extends a helping hand to us. It's ok when WE are doing the giving. We are in control. It is humbling to acknowledge that we might need some help. It doesn't mean we just let people wait on us. We are not helpless. But it does mean that we humbly accept the assistance people offer us. It is not easy to accept these gifts from others. We would rather be on the giving side. But we know that givers have to have receivers. How do we react when someone says "Can I help?" Are we quick to answer, "I can do it, thanks anyway." Or do we let that person minister to us no matter how big or small the gesture. Are we gracious recipients? Are we willing to have someone else wash our feet? Are we willing to let God wash our feet?

Pitcher and Basin used for the washing of feet on Holy Thursday

"And God saw how good it was." Genesis 1:19

Every so often, God gives us a blatant show of his creativity. And this is one of his "shows". Watching the rising of this moon over the waters of the Atlantic Ocean was awesome. As the big ball crept over the horizon, you had to wonder at the marvelous mystery of creation. The moon with its craters, the orbit it takes around the earth every twenty-four hours, the earth and its orbit aligning the two celestial bodies, the sun reflecting on the moon at just the certain point! How can this be? How can there not be a God?

If God can create such beautiful visions, with how much more care and love is his creation of us, who are made in his image. Sometimes we need to be reminded of his love for us. Moon risings promise his super care, signs of hope that God is in charge of all his creation. As the quote goes, "Let go and Let God!

Moon Rise over the Atlantic Ocean, Jensen Beach FL

It was a relaxing afternoon sitting there on the balcony of a friend's apartment. Facing the edge of the woods, the trees were almost within touching distance. Birds flited from branch to branch. The silence was pleasant, broken only by the rustle of leaves and the symphony of bird songs. It was a time to listen, to listen to the quiet, to listen to birdsong. It was a time to listen to the inner voice of God speaking. It was just being in the moment and knowing God is with me. A perfect time for prayer.

These moments are not always possible. We live at such a hectic pace; noise is a constant companion; our thoughts ramble through our heads, seemingly with no definite destination; there seems to be a constant demand for our time and attention. Finding even a short moment seems beyond our reach. How, in heaven's name, does one find quiet, or even the time to enjoy it? To have a "God moment" requires a deliberate choice on our part. God is here, waiting for us to choose to listen. It has to be deliberate because everything around us conspires against it. One must want a space of quiet strongly enough to go in search for it. It is "for heaven's sake" that we take time each day to find a quiet space to listen to the "quiet, still voice" of our God speaking within us. The question remains: Do you want this enough to make the choices that allow you the time and place?

"Let us be silent that we may hear the whisper of God."

RW Emerson

God Moment presented by a red cardinal

"Change is nothing to whine about."
Anon

Yes, these are wine vats stacked up at a winery in Napa Valley. Not the most beautiful photo but it holds a lot of promise. These vats speak of "transition". The fruit juice stored in them is in a state of flux even if we cannot see its action. Grape juice on its way to becoming a famous Napa Valley wine! We are all in some stage of transition even if unaware of it. Today is different from yesterday; tomorrow will be different than today. Some people call it "change", I prefer "Transition". We have many transitions in our lives as we move from one way of being to another. In some ways we hope for nothing to change, and in others we can't wait for a change to occur. Transition is an attitude of mind, a way of thinking that can offer an optimistic outlook on our lives. It is a gradual moving of who we are into another place. God is in these transition moments, opening us up to new possibilities, holding us when it seems the going is too much. These moments of change are holy moments whether they are large or small. They call us into taking who we have been into who we can be. We can't stand still. Day by day we continue to become the person we are meant to be, even if we don't realize it. Praise God for the wondrous ways he has led us to become who we are meant to be – a child of God.

Napa Valley wine coming to a shelf near you!

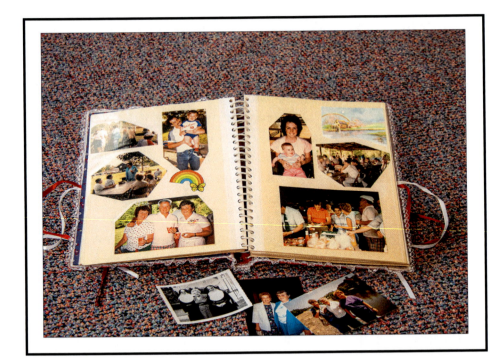

> *"Life has changed, not ended."*
>
> *Roman Ritual*

"When someone you love becomes a memory, your memories become your treasure." Several years ago, someone sent me a card with these words. Every time I experience a loss, the quote comes back to me. The loss of someone we love is hard. There are no two ways about it. We deeply miss the physical presence of the person we cared so much about. When our grieving diminishes a little bit, we realize that we hold in our hearts some wonderful memories, priceless treasures. I name these memories "the photo album of my heart." We each have one. It is an album that holds the moments, the stories, the times spent with our loved one. It is not an album that we can hold in our hands but one held in our hearts. It holds our treasures. And when our hearts are hurting, we can go to that album and choose a treasure that brings our loved one to the heart's mind. Sometimes we may weep a bit, and sometimes we may laugh. But the treasure is there for us to take. This is one of the ways that God helps to heal the soul and to give life to our spirit. And when possible, share that treasure with another so that they too may remember.

A glimpse into the old photo album

I love spring! It is my favorite season. Spring brings joy and lightness to my heart. It is a season of miracles. What was not so long ago lifeless, brown, withered, seemingly dead has come to new life. God has brought his paintbrush to our northern hemisphere and has colored our world with such wonderful shades of greens, pinks, yellows, purples, blues. Spring speaks to us of the love of a God who will not allow us to sit in the grays of a cold winter. And it has truly been a miserable winter. Not so much because of snow and ice, but because of the turmoil in our world. It is easy to get stuck in the mud of fear, discontent, hatred, prejudice, judgement. But God isn't going to let us wallow in the dark grays and browns that color our winters. No, God tells us that we are his beloved ones. He is present with us. He is not going to leave us to the wiles of sin and evil. Listen to what spring shouts out: New Life, New Hope. God is with us to help us not by erasing the things that weigh us down but by filling our hearts and minds with touches of his love that help us to move forward to the promises of Spring. God is speaking to us, to you and to me. Look at the miracles of each day, each new leaf that buds, each new flower that blooms. Even the dandelions shout out the wonders of our God.

Tulip bed, Highland Park, Rochester, NY

"There are miracles all around us."

Anon

> *"I will praise you among the people."*
>
> Ps. 108:4

Autumn's colors are bold and brassy. Oranges, golds, rusts, yellows. You just can't miss them in the garden. Even on the grayest fall days, they can't be hidden. In fact, it can be noted that when it is raining, the colors pop even more boldly. No fading wallflowers are these bright reminders of God's marvelous creativity. Do you recognize yourself in these colors? Do you continue to boldly flash God's mercy and love even on those dark and difficult days? Those days when we become discouraged because of the violence in our streets, even in our homes; the times when the evening news make us wonder if there will be any end to the wars, the poverty, the verbiage that slanders and detracts? Are you the "bright spot" that comes at the end of such news? Do you let your colors truly shout out? Mercy and Love are the tones of those colors. Because they are of God, they are bold and brassy in a world that prefers darkness. Remember that they are brightest when it is raining. Even if your spirit seems discouraged, pretend you are those colors. And in the pretending comes the reality.

Oranges and reds create fall beauty at the convent garden.

They are called "Messengers", messengers from God. "Behold! For I bring you good news of great joy, which will be to all people." And, having delivered the happy message, they burst into joyful song: "Glory to God in the highest, and peace to his people on earth."

Ah, Angels. Angels are not limited to the Christmas story, they are all around us. Do we hear their message? Do we rejoice in what they say? Who has been an angel bringing God's message of joy and hope to you? Was it the cashier at the grocery who wished you a good day? Or the child who offered a hug and a smile? The mailman who greeted you at the door? The friend who listened to the story of your mishap at work, the clerk at the store who took the time to find the item you were looking for? Ah, so many angels! Look to your day to see where the angels appeared. It raises the question: When were you an angel for someone else today? What opportunities did you take advantage of to bring the "tidings of joy and hope"? For it is in our concern and caring for one another that we are the messengers of God's good news. We bring messages of hope and love, and for that, we give "Glory to God in the highest." Rejoice in the fact that "you are an angel."

"Angels we have heard on high."

Luke 2:14

Angels highlight the Christmas tree.

"It is a happy talent to know how to play."

RW Emerson

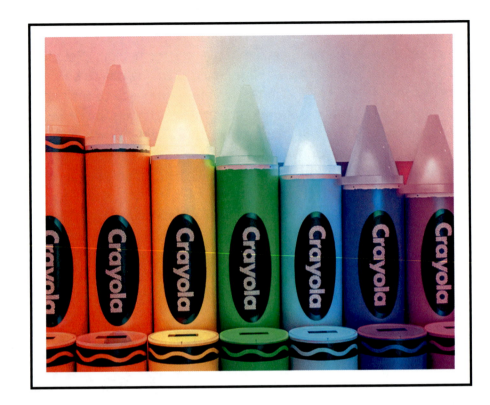

Who didn't appreciate a brand new box of crayons? What wonders would come out of that box? This lineup of colors can be found at the Strong Museum of Play's new interactive playground. Simply by waving your hand over the short stubs of color, one can create a variety of sounds and melodies. Raising your hand up and down gives levels of intensity in the tone. Creativity knows no bounds!

Stuart Brown, MD states that "Play keeps us fit physically and mentally." When was the last time you played? Really played? Play isn't just for little ones. It is for adults as well. When we play, we let go of the tensions and stresses inside us; we become mentally involved in the act of playing. We do it just for the fun of it. And we don't do enough of it. Playing opens up all sorts of creativity. As a child, give me a piece of paper, a box of crayons, a pair of scissors and I was all set for hours. Was this possibly the start of my adult "playing" that comes out of a black box called a camera? As we have grown older, perhaps the physical part of playing has diminished but there are still many great ways to play. Play is what we do "just for the fun of it." Anyone up for a good game of dominoes?

Human-sized Inter-active play at the Strong Museum of Play, Rochester, NY

"A time to scatter stones, and a time to gather them." Eccl 3:5

They look like just an ordinary pile of rocks. Called a "cairn", the ancients used them as road maps to get to their destination. Long before paved highways, certain configurations of rocks were left along side the narrow trails and paths to guide the traveler along the way. They showed the direction one should travel to their destination: left, right, straight ahead. These days we have a GPS and/or a road map (do they still print them?) to get us where we want to go. Looking at this cairn, it occurred to me that this would be a good symbol for the faith journey of a person, especially one's prayer. Naming my rocks Praise, Adoration, Gratitude, Forgiveness, Intercessions, all balanced on a firm foundation of Faith, give good direction to my prayer. They don't need to be big boulders. Simple stones will do it. Nor does the order in which they are stacked matter. Their direction leads upward, as incense rises up in our prayer. Sitting in my prayer space, the cairn gives me a reminder of how I ought to go about my prayer. And if they topple over, we can just stack them up again as a reminder that our faith journey is a road still in progress.

Cairn along Route 1A, New Hampshire

Spring is a season of openings. The buds on the trees are beginning to unfurl, the ground opens up to allow new life to emerge from dark and deep soil. Flowers start to unfold their petals to expose the center of their beings. Did you ever notice how new life starts to grow out from the center, from the core of the plant? In this Easter lily, the open petals draw our eyes to its center. There we can see the source of the color that radiates out to capture our attention. There we find the elements of the flower that ensure the growth of the flower into future generations. An open flower is a thing of wonder.

What of ourselves? Can we envision ourselves opening up our center? What is there determines the growth and beauty of the flower. Goodness radiates out when God is at the Center of our lives. We can no longer deny what we are called to be. Our Source of being gives us what we need to be that person God has destined us to be. As we watch spring unfold, let us not hesitate to unfurl our petals and radiate to others the compassion and mercy of our Creator God.

"Our hearts can always be in the same place, centered in God."

C. McAuley

Spring at the Lamberton Conservatory, Rochester, NY

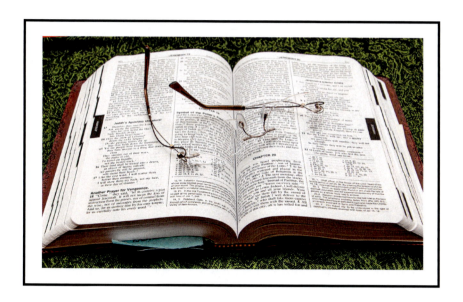

" Some things have to be believed to be seen."   RW Emerson

2020! When that new year began, we found the words "twenty, twenty" to roll off our tongues easily because we are so used to saying them. 20/20 is how we describe perfect vision. Literally, 20/20 means we see clearly, everything is in focus, colors are sharp. When this changes, we begin to wear glasses or contacts so we can see clearly again. We have cataracts removed. We do what we need to do in order to see clearly.

Figuratively, 20/20 vision could refer to our inner vision. How clearly do we "see" what is around us? Within us? In our minds and in our hearts? What do we need to do to sharpen that vision, to re-focus? Like the eye exam, we need to examine ourselves to see where we are blinded. Is it in our relationships with others? Our relationship with the Creator who gave us our 20/20 vision? Are our eyes shut to the needs of people around us? Close-minded to the things that cause climate change? What do you need to do to improve your vision? It is not by chance that the glasses are resting on the words of Scripture. This is the place to start. You will find the prescription for "new glasses" found within its pages.

The Bible and glasses waiting in my prayer space

"Be imitators of God."

Ephesians 5:1

Jery Taylor is a "culture bearer". At the age of 5, her grandmother and mother taught her how to weave the sweetgrass baskets that have come to represent her Gullah culture. the Gullah people living in the Low Country of South Carolina, first came to the US from West Africa in the slave trade of the 1600's. They brought their skill of basket weaving with them. Jery is one who works diligently to keep alive the cultural traditions of her Gullah people.

A "culture bearer" is one who brings the heritage of one's nationality to the attention of others. Ours is the culture given to us because of our faith in God. This is the Culture that transcends all other cultures. It calls us to work for justice and peace, to love our neighbors, to share with one another, to seek the good for others. It invites us to leave behind the negative cultures that promote hatred and poverty. We became a part of this God-Culture when we professed our belief in the faithfulness of an ever-loving Creator, and when we live the values inherent to our faith. When and where and how today might you bring the inherent joy of belonging to God's Culture to another? Are we not Christ-bearers?

Jery's woven basket in Charleston, GA

We need to celebrate "Earth Day". Really celebrate it! It is not just a date on the calendar to remind us of the beauty and complexity of the earth. It is not just a call to action by a few environmentalists who are sounding the alarm. It is a sign of Hope. There are so many different issues that need to be addressed that one can become overwhelmed: Water, Air, earth, and hundreds of branches of these elements. It is a sign of Hope because this pandemic we have gone through shows us that if we work together globally, we can overcome the issues that threaten us. If we can work together to contain this virus, it will show that we are able to work together to correct the issues of our environment. We can't do everything but we can do something. Choose one or two issues that attract you, things that you know you can do something about. Read up on it, reflect on the actions that will help change the way you think about it, and put the actions into practice. Vote for people who see the environment as a major concern. The covid-19 virus is showing us that we can make a difference. Together we can make a difference in protecting God's creation. Happy Earth Day!

"Be glad and rejoice forever in what I create."

Isaiah 65:18

Small pond hidden in the side streets of Irondequoit, NY

"Happy the people whose God is the Lord."

Ps 144:15

This quote from Pope Francis caught my attention: "Lent is a time of repentance, not of sorrow. It is a time of penance but not of sorrow, of mourning".
We tend to make these 40 days of Lent as a time of gloom. To be happy and joyful seems to be out of place. I've always felt funny about saying I was looking forward to Lent. Who in their right mind would think that! Yes, Lent is a time to do what I need to do in order to straighten out my pathway to fully being a Christian. And this means doing things that we call penance. Ceasing to do things that keep me from following Christ and doing things that help me to follow him more closely doesn't necessarily mean I have to wear a long face. Lent is not a time of doom and gloom. It is a prelude to the wondrous event of Jesus' death and resurrection by which he redeemed us from an eternity without God. So, when you are eating tuna noodle casserole for the fifth time in five weeks, do it with joy in your heart because we are an Easter People, an Alleluia People! We have good reason to be joyful and peaceful.

Lent - Daffodils at Eastman House Dutch Bulb display

Highland Park is the home to over 1500 lilac bushes of varying colors and size. While it has become a tradition for me to visit the Park at least once during the spring season, intuitively I know that it is never the same. This year's blooms are not the same as last year's. The colors may be brighter or less intense. The shape of the blooms differ. So, while the destination is the same, it is still different. What was last year is not this year's vision.

So too we are different from last year. We can never return to the person we were before the pandemic. For some it will be in major ways: a loved one lost; we may have been sick ourselves; or have lost our job and now are in a new one. But all of us have been affected in small ways. Our spirits may have changed, our awareness of others around us may have been intensified as we reached out to the lonely and elderly in different ways. We may have found ways to make do without things we have taken for granted. Perhaps our spiritual growth has changed as we sought new ways to pray because we couldn't gather as a faith community. Maybe we have found ourselves grumpier, and complaining. Whoever we are now is not the same as we were a year ago. There is always opportunity for a new photograph of the person we have become. Like the lilacs, we are a new creation. What will your picture look like?

Lilacs in Highland Park, Rochester, NY

"Nature is a friend you can visit anytime."

Anon

"May God make you the instrument of his glory."

C. McAuley

Gazing around as I sat in my beach chair, I noticed little points of light reflecting in the grains of sand. Little flakes of the mineral mica catching the sun's shine. Some a little brighter than others but there none the less. They reminded me of other points of light. The lights of kind actions people have done for one another during the time of pandemic. We are tired of all things Covid but now is not the time to quit. We need to continue doing the little things that help make someone else's day a bit brighter. The little gestures of caring that are contagious and are passed on to touch the lives of others: a smile, a listening ear, a nod. a phone call, or a letter, a prayer for one who needs encouragement. It helps my spirit to recognize these points of light. They make me realize that I am not alone, that others are there for me. And it encourages me to be a point of light for someone else. Our actions may seem trivial to us but they mean much to someone else who receives them. Taking time at the end of the day to recognize the kindnesses and goodness that surrounds me reminds me of how wonderful people are. Like the multitude of tiny specks of mica on the beach, the points of light of our actions are all around us. Keep your eyes open for their appearances.

Lisette's beach chair on Hampton Beach, NH

Walking in the cemetery the other day I overheard Mama ghost talking to her baby ghost: "Remember, don't spook until you are spoken to." Ah, Halloween!

We can find much online about the origins of Halloween and it is fun to explore just how the traditions we now celebrate have evolved. Let's just say that it is vastly different ftom how the Irish once celebrated it centuries ago. Do you remember the first time you went trick or treating without your parents? And when you dumped your bag of goodies on the table? (one neighbor always gave us pencils. Pencils!) Or how about the decision of what you were going to be? The more outlandish the better! Halloween is a fun celebration that we need right now. The dressing up in costumes gives us a period of time to pretend that all is right with the world. And the door to door "trick or treating" allows us to hide the fears of covid 19. So put on your mask and grab your pumpkin bag and call out "trick or treat!"

"It's a happy talent to know how to play." — RW Emerson

Halloween display in the neighborhood

"The earth, the sea, and the air are the concern of every nation."

John F. Kennedy

Realizing that most of my photographs are of the natural world, I have gathered them under the umbrella of a single title, "Reverence the Earth". Webster defines "reverence" as "a feeling or attitude of deep respect, love and awe for something sacred". The Earth is our sacred space. We are standing on holy ground. Some might think that to reverence the earth is akin to worshipping every tree, river, mountain as a god. The tree is not God. Nor is the river or mountain. They are creations of a generous God who has invited us to name every plant, tree and animal and to have dominion over them. But our "dominion" is in the call to respect the gifts we have been given, to be stewards of this planet earth, to treat earth with awe, not to destroy and obliterate. When we show respect for the Gift, then we are honoring the Giver. And so, we care for creation, our mother earth. We each have a part in her welfare. Individually and collectively we can make a difference in each of our own personal sacred grounds. We can't leave it for someone else to do. Being aware of what we can do is not enough. We have to put it into action. My photographs are meant to be reminders that God's created beauty is all around us. Everyday should be Earth Day, a day in which we do something to better the sad conditions we have imposed on it. Go on, go out, go reverence the earth. We Can Do It!

Sunset at Sea Breeze, NY captured in ball

Something interesting is happening on the streets, maybe I should say, on the walls of Rochester. You may have noticed as you travel down the streets that there is a lot of "wall therapy" going on. These are not your usual graffiti. Portraits of well-known and not so well-known people have been painted on walls of buildings around the city. Landscapes, abstracts, messages, people at work, play or just hanging out. Animals, flowers. Signs of caring, loving, hope for one another. Well over a hundred drab brick walls have come to life and have brightened up one's day.

Just about 10 years ago, Dr Ian Wilson wanted to repay the city of Rochester for all it had done for him. His thank you took the form of what is now called "wall therapy". It is a project of displaying communal art by transforming walls, buildings and neighborhoods into expressions of the local community. Armed with spray cans of paint, brushes, ladder, tarps and many onlookers, they have accomplished works of art that inspire many. Imagine having a brick wall 15' by 20' as your canvas! This project has been recognized by over 2000 cities and has had visitors from around the world hoping to start similar projects in their home towns. This has truly been a project that has sparked inspiration in individuals and communities alike. Isn't it just amazing that such beauty can be created by a can of spray paint. Thank you to all the artists who have shared their gift of with us.

"Everyone needs beauty as well as bread."
John Muir

Wall therapy in downtown Rochester, NY

Almost ready to open, the sunflower pod promises a gift of bright color. The new yellow petals look like little hands playing peek-a-boo, shyly hiding the package of seeds within. Even the process of unfolding is a gift of beauty. The intricate details of the leaves, their symmetry, their allowing of a peek at the golden insides…who but a loving creator can design such a thing. As the sunflower evolves into what it is meant to be, each phase of its unfolding is a picture of wondrous beauty. The glory of its full sunflower status is not the fulfillment of what it is called to be. It doesn't end there. Besides giving us the sunshine of its golden petals, it continues its life cycle by providing pollen for the bees, seeds for the birds (and humans), and disperses seeds for next year's cycle of life. Like this sunflower, we, too, are constantly unfolding. Each good thing we do, each kind word we speak, each prayer we utter is not the end of who we are called to be. As life evolves for each one of us, every day is a new opportunity to show forth the glory of our Creator God.

"Shout joyfully to God, all you on earth."

Ps. 66:1

Sunflower waiting to open, Rt. 65, Mendon, NY

"Come see the works of God."

Ps. 66:5

The sunflower pod has opened. Did you even imagine such beauty? My mind boggles to see such a demonstration of God's creativity and love. Just look at the intricate detail. The tiny seeds that will feed the finch and other small birds. Hidden in the small flowerets is a busy little bee gathering pollen for the hive. How wonderfully made the sunflower is! When Jesus tells us to "consider the lilies of the field," we must consider also ourselves. How wonderfully are we made! With the intricate details of who we are, we too reflect the sunshine of God's glory. Like the sunflowers of the field where no two are identical, no two of us are alike and that makes for a wonderfully diverse garden. May each of us reflect the glory of God to all those who inhabit our garden. Praise God for these summer wonders of his creation that give us so much joy.

Opened Sunflower, Rt. 65, Mendon, NY

The "work of human hands" is what we celebrate this Labor Day. God uses our "human hands" to continue his work of creation. Take these grapes for example. Using what God has given us, grapes are transformed into a wonderful drink or one of the Naples, NY's famous grape pies. The vine dressers work long hours to bring this fruit to its fullness. Many hands go into the food chain to enable us to eat and/or drink the fullness of the grapes. Each of us has received the gift of work, the ability to transform the ordinary into extraordinary. Whether it is physical labor, mental work, or spiritual work, we use the gifts/talents with which a gracious God has blessed us. We use our human hands to bring these blessings to others. Every work we do, however insignificant or tedious, is a blessing to others. The "work of our hands" is transformed when we offer that work to the Lord. Start each day with a prayer that the work of your hands will be done for the honor and glory of God. Your work then becomes a "holy work", a prayer offered to God, a blessing for all who receive the work of your hands. Let every day be a labor day of love, transforming the ordinary into God's extraordinary.

"Blessed are you, Lord, God of all creation ...

... for through your goodness we have received the wine that we offer you, the fruit of the vine and the work of human hands ..."

(Offertory prayer from Roman Missal)

Vineyard along Seneca Lake, Seneca County

"I will bless the Lord at all times."

Ps. 34:1

There is no question about it. We lead very busy, active lives. Even those of us who are "retired" find that we are always busy about something. At the end of the day, we wonder where the time went. One of the most important actions of our day often becomes the one we put off the easiest. Prayer. No one can doubt the importance of taking specific time each day to converse with our God. Yet, when the end of the day comes, unless it has become a priority, prayer is that which is left undone. Prayer, some may say, is something I will catch up on when I am sick or forced to be inactive. Well, having just recuperated from a bout of covid, let me assure you that when you are sick prayer is the last thing your mind wants to consider. Yes, offering the discomfort of having a temperature, aches, and other things that come with illness can be considered prayer. But our bodies tell us that this is not what it wants to do. The mind and heart just can't focus on listening to what God is speaking to us. So, don't wait to cultivate the practice of daily prayer. Being a prayerful person prepares us for those times when prayer is hard to do. Pray without ceasing during your days now. Don't put it off.

Path through the woods leading to Chimney Bluffs, Sodus Point, NY

This Psalm verse is a reminder to me that I will find God's love and care in the midst of my day. To believe is to be convinced that this will happen, that I can see this in the people and events of my day if I but take the time to recognize the Lord's presence in the so called "daily grind." Where do I find the goodness of the Lord? Where else but in the "land of the living", among those who also believe, who are living the Gospel. I expect to find the Lord there. But I also need to look for God's goodness in the midst of the uglier parts of life as well. With the eyes of faith, I will catch glimpses of the Lord where I don't expect to see him – in the person who is angry, hurting or grieving, the family struggling to keep it all together, in the disasters that occur in nature, in the war-torn countries, in the perils of poverty and racism, in the abuse of our earthly home. It may take a while to see God there but he will reveal himself in the many different ways that are signs of his goodness. Lord, bless my eyes that they may see!

Irondequoit Bay at Franklin Park, Webster, NY

"I believe that I shall see the goodness of the Lord in the land of the living."

Ps 27:14.

"Take heart all you who hope in the Lord."
Ps. 31:25

It has taken longer than usual this year for the colors of fall to appear. This stunning tree glows even though the skies are gray. Some of its leaves already are leaving a golden carpet on the still-green grass. As its present life cycle spins into the process of ending, it shouts out a reminder that a new cycle of life is beginning. For me, this is a sign of hope. Our Creator-God promises a spring time of new life. Yes, there will be months of barrenness, apparent emptiness when nothing seems to be happening. But already there is new growth as future leaves begin to push off the old, readying the tiny nodules that will form new growth. The tree will, unobservable to our human eye, almost secretly, continue growth. Hope, to me, is like this. Sometimes it may feel as though nothing will ever change; I may feel an emptiness but still there is a longing, a yearning for goodness to happen. It may feel as if God has left me, left us, as prayers appear to not being heard. Like the tree, God is at work even if we don't recognize it. "May the God of hope fill you with all joy and peace in believing, so that by the power of the Holy Spirit you may abound in hope." Romans 15:13

Ginkgo tree on Blossom Road, Rochester, NY

"It is the smallest of all seeds."

Matthew 13:32

Have you planted any mustard seeds lately? Any time is a good time for dropping these tiny little seeds into the ground. Jesus tells us that these tiniest of seeds can grow into the largest of bushes. Google tells us that the Middle Eastern mustard tree reaches a height of about 25 feet and can be as wide as it is tall. From just a little seed! So, have you planted any of these tiny little seeds? They are the seeds of kindness, generosity, peace, love, hope. We can drop them anywhere. We can plant them in the lives of those with whom we live, work, worship, we can drop them at the grocery store, walking along the street, in our neighborhoods, even on Facebook!. We can plant all year round. Be aware of the potential of each little seed. The harvesting of the mustard plant gives us that wonderful spice that flavors our foods. We may never know the spices that result from our seedings but we are confident that the Lord sees the mighty trees that come from those seeds of hope, love, peace. Go plant some seeds today!

Not a mustard bush but about the size of one.

Table after table, stacked high with things no longer wanted by their owners. Ah, yes, the Next to New Sale at a local parish. Viewing this vast assortment of things available for a very small cost, I wondered how high the mountain would be if it were all tossed into a land fill. Those summer garage/yard sales are doing their part to keep from adding to the vast assortment of things that just get tossed out. Down-sizing may clean out our attics but does it have to mean just adding what we don't want into our landfills where it may take centuries to decompose? What have you unthinkingly tossed into the trash today? Could you have done something with it, maybe repurposed it, taken it to the recycling bin where it could be disposed of properly? Sure, it takes an extra bit of work to be thoughtful about what we throw out so casually, but every little thing can add or subtract from the environment's sustainability. So, let's hear it for all those who have donated or worked hard to put together these garage sales. After all, they could have just tossed these things to the curb.

"To know you have enough is to be rich."

Tao

Next to New Sale at Blessed Sacrament Church, Rochester, NY

"Grace and mercy are with his holy ones."

Wisdom 3:9

The mirror surface of the pond reflects the beauty of the fall as the day nears a close. A quiet moment offers some thoughts about the many who have this cemetery as their resting place. My parents and many relatives lie in peace in this place. Like the reflecting colors of fall in the water, we each carry with us a reflection of the goodness and love of the person we knew. We are a reflection of the one we love. Certainly, we carry away a physical resemblance. My Dad had curly, wavy hair. So do I. But I hope I carry with me his faith and his love of God and the patience that he displayed, especially his patience with his students in his classroom. Our loved ones live on in us. We remember them through the imitation of the qualities that made them the special person they were. We reflect that quality to others. Not always perfectly. As the ripples in the water gives the trees a bit of a different look, we put our own touch to the reflections. We pray that one day our lives will be reflected in the ones we love who come after us. Identify what gift your loved one shared with you and live a life that passes that gift on to others. What gift will you pass on?

Reflecting pond at Holy Sepulchre Cemetery, Rochester, NY

Pitch black envelops you as you drive along the shore line for about a mile. One side hides a lake you cannot see, the other side, a park. Such is the intensity of the darkness. However, as you round a slight bend in the road, you are startled out of the darkness by a wonderful display of Christmas lights: Trees laden with lights, a house outlined in golden bulbs and a driveway edged in brightness. It takes your breath away.

We don't like the dark. We complain "it gets dark so soon". Yet, we know there will be an increase of light as we go through the solstice. We are in spiritual darkness as well, overwhelmed by all that is going on in our world, in our cities, our families. Our faith gives us hope that this darkness, too, will come to an end and this hope will lighten our days.

And then, on December 25th, we hear from John 1:5 "A Light shines in the darkness and the darkness grasped it not." There is no darkness so dark that it can overcome the Light who is the Christ. This Light is Emmanuel, God with us. This is the end of Advent, of waiting. Be startled by the Light that is with us. Let it take your breath away!

"A light shines in our darkness."

John 1:15

Light display, Lakeshore Blvd, Irondequoit, NY

Peace! This is our desire for the New Year, our wish, our hope, our prayer. Unfortunately, it seems to be the most elusive gift to obtain. Perhaps it is because we look at peace as being the absence something: an end to war, freedom from strife, an end of violence. And all of this seems to be something out of our reach, out of our ability to acquire. But the dictionary offers other meanings to the word "Peace": a calm, a quiet, stillness, tranquility, harmony. Is it possible to have this kind of peace? Certainly. But it requires a bit of work on our part. That work is to bring ourselves to the Center of who we are. We must clear our lives of that which causes a lack of peace: those distractions and anxieties that limit our ability to recognize that we are, in St. John's words, "the children of God." This mean that we must keep God first and center in our lives. Our choices must be faith-filled, righteous, honorable, just, and based on the great commandment to love God with our whole heart, mind, will, and to love our neighbor as ourselves. This brings peace to our hearts. And a heart filled with peace spills that peace out to those we encounter in our day. Maybe, if we all work at our inner peace we will be able to effect peace in others. A blessed, God-filled, peace-filled New Year to you.

"Peace be with you, my friend."

Christmas ornament

"In the name of the Father, and of the Son, and of the Holy Spirit."

Shamrocks or clover? Both are used to symbolize good luck. The Shamrock has three leaves and grows in clumps, while the clover has four, and are rarer and are harder to find. Legend has it that St. Patrick himself used the shamrock as a visual to describe the inter-connectiveness of the Blessed Trinity: Father, Son, Spirit. Three in one. Three parts of the one shamrock. It was a common visual, one the Irish could relate to. The shamrock became associated with the Irish people and Saint Patrick after his time, and it has maintained its place in Irish culture ever since. But the clover also has a long history in Ireland. The Druids used clover to ward off evil. Even though the Druids no longer exist, the four leafed clover is thought to also bring luck. Still, the shamrock holds the place of honor when it comes to celebrating all things Irish. Perhaps it is because it speaks of the very foundation of the Christian faith that Patrick brought to Ireland, the mystery of the Blessed Trinity. But perhaps we might look at the clover with its four parts of one plant as the three parts being the Trinity, and the fourth being ourselves who have become one with the Father, Son and Spirit through our baptism into the life of the Trinity. Certainly not a theological truth but a sign of our being at one with the God of all creation.

Street lights along the streets of Dublin, Ireland

*"Be holy,
for I,
the Lord your God,
am holy."*

Leviticus 19:1

This is the work of Lent: to "be holy". And that, we admit, seems to be an enormous task, one we are tempted to ignore because, after all, who can presume to be holy like God. But there it is, in black and white before us in the Hebrew scriptures. Be holy. God wants for us to be holy. Being holy is a daily process. We will not wake up tomorrow holy and that is it for the rest of our life. Each day we practice holiness so that it becomes who we are. Each day is a new start to our journey of holiness. None of us is perfect. We will come to roadblocks that will make us wonder if we even know how to be holy. The Lord tells us what we need to do to imitate him. Matthew's gospel spells it out loud and clear. To be holy as our heavenly Father is holy, we reach out from our selflove to love our neighbors. "Whatever you do to the least of my brothers and sisters you do to me." That is where our holiness lies – in what we do for one another. Feed the hungry, clothe the naked, shelter the homeless. We know what we have to do, we just need to get about doing it. Lent is a time to renew our efforts. Our mission is to be holy.

A quiet stroll down a residential street in East Aurora, NY yesterday revealed a glimpse of the spirit of community that is present in this small western New York town. Many yards hosted a platter-sized red heart mounted on a wire frame. People began placing them in their yards and businesses when the pandemic of Covid 19 began to show its face along with the need to quarantine. A lady sitting on her porch gave me the story. The distribution of the hearts was initiated by a gentleman who was concerned by the isolation people were facing. The hearts were to be a reminder for neighbors to look out for neighbors. It was an invitation to show caring love to those around us. While the pandemic has lessened, the hearts still stand to encourage the residents to continue the spirit of community. And added to some of the hearts is now a heart of blue and yellow reminding us of the need to include other neighborhoods and countries in the scope of our attention and prayer. The Ukraine's colors stand next to the red hoping that the Ukrainians realize that we are standing with them. Would that we all had hearts in our yards.

"May love surround you, faith sustain you, hope encourage you."

Anon

Yard signs on lawns in East Aurora, NY

"You are precious in my eyes and I love you." Isaiah 43:4

The season for this beautiful iris has come to an end. A late May/early June flower, it transitions us into the colors of summer. There is something about this flower that attracts me. Perhaps it is the softness of its peach color, or the way it stands tall and sturdy on its slender stem. It may be the way it slowly unfolds from a tight bud. Or just simply because it is there. What is your favorite garden flower. What attracts you to its beauty?

Our relationships with others are often like this. There is a certain something about the other that makes us that wants us to know more about them. It doesn't matter if they are a regal iris or a lowly dandelion. There are special qualities in each of us that give us our personal beauty. Sometimes it takes awhile for one's beauty to be revealed but when it is, it can be breathtaking. God sees the beauty in each of us. It is said, "Beauty is in the eye of the beholder." God's eyes are always upon us and what God sees is our beauty, our inner beauty. Can we see how God is attracted to us? We are his creation, He is never distracted away from us. Praise God who has filled us with every good thing.

Iris in a neighbor's garden

What? You don't recognize this picture of the wind? Jesus told Nicodemus that "the wind blows where it wills. You hear the sound it makes but you do not know where it comes from or where it goes."

When I was about 3 years old and spending the night at my aunt's house, there was a very strong wind that was shaking the whole house. And as it blew, all the little doo-dads on my aunt's dresser were knocking together. And the house creaked as the wind whistled at the windows. To a three year old, this can be quite scary. As a result I have always minded the strong winds. So I can identify with those gathered in the upper room who witnessed the powerful winds that blew outside on Pentecost. We don't see wind, but we see its effects in the natural world around us. In the scriptures, wind is synonymous with the Holy Spirit. Don't be afraid of the Wind of the Spirit. It may shake us but it will move us to a new Way of living, the Way of Jesus.

"The wind blows where it will."
John 13:8

Wind blown clouds at Sea Breeze beach on Lake Ontario

"Where flowers bloom, so does hope" (Lady Bird Johnson).

A few years back, the caretakers of Holy Sepulchre Cemetery in Rochester planted daffodil bulbs, thousands of them, at the headstones of the priests and sisters buried there. Each year since then the cluster of daffodils has grown as the bulbs multiply in the dark earth. A springtime carpet of yellow once again brings a smile as we recognize the hope these early bloomers give. Hope is that inner yearning for what is not yet. We all have hopes and wishes. But what is our ultimate hope? The daffodils at the graves remind us that those who lie here in the ground have had their ultimate hope fulfilled. Faith has given them that hope, the hope that they will be enjoying the everlasting life of being with their God, that they now live in the ultimate hope of Love.. These little blooms bowing and dancing in the breeze shout out that the ultimate hope of the priests and sister buried there has been fulfilled. They are in the presence of God, who is Love. What is your ultimate hope?

Religious Sisters burial grounds at Holy Sepulchre Cemetery, Rochester, NY

> *"If you love nature, you will find beauty everywhere."*
>
> V. VanGogh

I watched the snow dance outside my window last night. The building's night security light cast a golden tone as the flakes danced up and down, swirling and gliding, bowing and swerving to the music of the wind. The Dance would slow as the wind changed tempo, only to grow in intensity as the snow from the roof added to the choreography. Mesmerized, I never even thought to pick up a camera to capture the dance. But it wouldn't have mattered, the dance is in my mind. It was one of those "God moments", a moment in time that lets you know that God is in the here and now. I let the camera in my heart memorize the picture. The Dance is over now, the music of the wind has quieted the snow. I am waiting for the encore, the next snow dance. Isn't it wonderful to have a window through which to see life. What do you see from your window?

The south hill behind the Mercy Center in Rochester, NY

"And the greatest of these is Love."

1 Cor 13:13

Caution: Beach Artist at Work! Have you ever wondered how the heart became the symbol of Love? Its roots go back to centuries before Christ. The Greek philosophers had a common agreement that the emotions rested in the heart. Love was considered the strongest of all emotions (hate, anger, fear, etc.) St. Paul says "the greatest of these is Love". In the 14th century, the first images of a heart reflecting love were used.

But it is more important to know what Love is, rather than the icon we use. Love is a strong emotion and true love focuses not so much on the lover but the one who is being loved. Love is a deliberate act of caring for someone more than you care for yourself. Love is wanting the good for others, wanting the best for them. We know that God made us to love and to be loved. We know God loves us. But God is love. And this means that God is continuously valuing us more than himself. So much so that he chose to die on the cross for love of us. This is perfect love. It is the love we strive to have. St. John tells us: "For whoever does not love their brother and sister, whom they have seen, cannot love God, whom they have not seen. He has given us this command: Anyone who loves God must also love their brother and sister." 1 John 4:19-20. It is in our day to day, year in, year out displays of love, that show the true depths of our love.

Sand sculpture on the beach at Mercy by the Sea, CT

The colors of winter are monochromatic: shades of grays and browns, touched now and then by the whiteness of snow. Usually by mid-February in the northern hemisphere, we have become a bit tired of this colorless world. Our hearts and spirits yearn for color.. But sometimes that promise seems late in coming. The winters of covid have dimmed whatever color there might have been. Tired of the pandemic, tired of the political back and forth, fearful of a world that is marked by violence, frustrated by a culture that lacks respect and courtesy toward one another, worried by the economy of the day, we cry out to God: "I've had it!" We long for the return of color to our lives. But do we realize that we ourselves are the ones who bring the color. Color comes from within us. The colors of our smiles shine into the gloom. The warmth of our kindnesses for others intensify the tones of our colors. Put aside the dark colors, wear something bright. Our faith in God's being with us gives the color of hope. Believing that God cares for us and living that belief changes the way we look at the colors of other who surround us. The world is not just the browns and grays, it is a rainbow of color. We are the colors of the rainbow. Be the color you are meant to be. Don't be afraid to show it off.

"How beautiful a day touched by kindness."
Anon

Dutch Bulb exhibit, George Eastman House, Rochester, NY

*"I think
that I shall never
see
a poem as lovely
as a tree."*

Joyce Kilmer

"My tree" stands alone in a side yard at the corner of a busy intersection. It's not tall and stately like the maples and oaks that overshadow it. But it is full, rather squatty and has a unique quality all its own. Its leaves change into amazing colors of oranges and red oranges. As they drop from the tree, they cover the ground with a carpet fit for the steps of a king. I call it the "starfish" tree because its leaves resemble a starfish, five sections to each leaf, with a little baby leaf thrown in for good measure. From the road you would never recognize its unique look. It is when you are up close and take the time to look that you are at a loss for words to describe this beauty. Sometimes all you can do is look: the light dancing through the leaves, the branches dividing the tree into sections, the music in the rustle of leaves, the texture of the brown bark, the flutter of a leaf as it drifts gently to the ground. Words cannot contain the breath-taking glory of this single tree. And you hold the memory in your heart. What do you see? What "trees' of beauty do you hold in the memory of your heart?"
Kilmer concludes his poem: "A poem is made by fools like me, but only God can make a tree."

"Starfish" tree leaf on Merchants Rd., Rochester, NY

This perfect blessing prayer reminds me that the Lord is indeed keeping me in his care. There are so many ways that my well-being has been touched by him. Just waking up in the morning is being blessed with another day of life. The Lord's face shines upon me through the events of my day, through the people present in my life, through the moments of interaction with the world about me, nature, the arts, loved ones. And the Lord is certainly most gracious to me when I have been less than who I am called to be. He forgives my lapses in being his child and continues to encourage me to be better. Yes, the Lord does look upon me kindly. And sometimes that feels like a divine hug. As I remember all the blessings the Lord has set upon me, I am at peace. Being with the Lord is being with Peace, the peace that the world cannot give me. Even more wondrously, I am able to be a bearer of the Lord's blessings for others. It is by my actions in serving others that I am an instrument of God's blessing for others. A blessing is a gift, a gift freely given. What a world it would be if we realized how we can bless others by calling upon the Lord to bless them. How do you describe how you have been blessed?

> "May the Lord bless you and keep you. The Lord let his face shine upon you and be gracious to you. The Lord look upon you kindly and give you peace!"
> Numbers 6:24-26

Butterfly, Portsmouth, NH garden.

Earth Day was first celebrated on April 22, 1970 in response to a recognition that we need to protect our environment from the many pollutants that are destroying its ecosystem. In 1990 it became a global event as many nations around the world acknowledged the work needed to save our planet. Celebrating this day serves to show us that there are many opportunities and ways for us to protect our planet home. Some are general, wide scope concerns like water, air pollution, refuse. And these seem overwhelming. But there are many smaller ways we can individually contribute to save our planet. Little things like being aware of how we might be wasting water, of our use of plastic. We may be only one person and wonder what difference I would make? Be assured, you make a big difference! If we all did one positive thing each day, just one, it is one more than yesterday. It is a way to praise the Lord: "Lord of all, to thee we raise/This our hymn of grateful praise."

"Attacks on nature have consequences for people's lives".

Bishops of the Amazon, SA

Wet lands along eastern seaboard.

"Spring is nature's way of saying, 'Let's party'"
Robin Williams

Exuberance is the color for the day. The world in our northern hemisphere is filled with mind blowing color. The yellows of the daffodils, pinks, reds, oranges of tulips, purple grape hyacinth, greens of new grass and leaves, yellow dots of dandelions in the lawn. Along with the budding blossoms on trees, who cannot help but feel a lifting up of their spirit. While out in the car this morning I saw a young girl, maybe eleven or twelve, crossing the street with a hop, skip and jump, filled with exuberance and fun, arms reaching high as if to capture the snowing petals. Her delight in the world around her shining in her face as she spun around at all she saw. Her spirit was contagious and made me more conscious of the beauty of creation along the way. It was a "wish I had my camera" moment. Even cloudy skies couldn't mask the glory of the sights. We have had so many "down" moments these past few years, it is time to open our eyes and look, to really see what is before us. Take some time this day, or tomorrow, and put your cares into the hands of the Lord. Simply say, "Lord, you've got this for a few moments." And let your heart wander to the color and sights of spring. New life is all around us. Don't miss it!

Tulip bed, Highland Park, Rochester, NY

"Christ lives in me."

Galations:2:20

In my early years of teaching first graders. when the day was over, we would stand facing the crucifix and pray for a safe journey home. One day, after we finished the prayer, Mary Jo came to my desk and said: "Sister, I've been thinking." (dangerous territory here!) "I've been thinking that we should look at each other when we pray because Jesus lives in each one of us. He's not really truly on the cross!" Wow! This is the Resurrection! This is the essence of our relationship with God! Jesus is no longer on the cross, nor in the tomb. He is Risen and lives among us, lives within us. Our Baptism tells us this. Our faith believes this. We say with St. Paul in his letter to the Galatians: "I live no longer I but Christ lives in me." And in you. In each one of us. Imagine the consequences if we all realized this. How this would change the world. Still wearing my teacher's hat, I asked Mary Jo what she thought would happen if we looked at each other during prayer. "We would laugh," she answered, realizing how it would work out. Yes, we would laugh. And we should laugh because of the joy of recognizing the miracle of the Resurrection. May we always seek the Risen Christ in each other. We are filled with joy.

Monument of the Resurrection at Holy Sepulchre Cemetery, Rochester, NY

What do I leave behind when I go away from the presence of another? Each of us leaves an impression however fleeting the encounter may be. The psalmist tells us that goodness and mercy follow us. Just as the perfume a person wears lingers after they are gone, so do mercy and goodness linger after us, follow after us, long after we are gone. Have we left behind a person changed even just a little because of our expressions of mercy and goodness?

The Church begins the season of Lent recognizing that God's Mercy and Goodness are with us. We have been changed by this realization, and we continue to be changed as we acknowledge how much God loves us. Lent gives an opportunity to practice letting Mercy and Goodness follow us. To practice means we haven't gotten it quite perfect so we keep trying to bring Mercy and Goodness to one another …all the days of our lives. A blessed Lent to you on your Lenten journey.

"Surely, Mercy and Goodness shall follow me, all the days of my life."

Ps. 23:6

Lent - blossoming tree in Seneca Falls, NY

During Covid-19, my cousin arrived at my door looking like a dog face. Well, from his nose to his chin he resembled the snout of a german shepherd. A delightful change from the powder blue mask that protected us from the virus. It has been a bit of entertainment to see the many creative face coverings people sported as we tried to make the best of a not-so-great situation. Having our face covered even part way sometimes gave us the feeling of anonymity. Folks didn't always recognize us. And so, many took the action of finding masks that said something about who they are. The woman in the check out line whose mask was a mix of alphabet letters showed that she was a primary school teacher. The sports teams we favor rose up on our faces. My niece favors aqua colored masks – her sacred color. Unicorns seemed to be more prevalent as were batman and the like. Cat and dog lovers. Hearts and flowers people. We could tell so much about a person by the mask they wore. Ah, the stories hiding behind these masks. What fun to trying to imagine what some of these stories are. Makes us look a little closer at each other, doesn't it.

"God made

you

one of a kind."

Anon.

Designer Masks I wore during Covid-19

*"Lord of hosts,
restore us;
Let your face
shine upon us that
we may be saved."*

Ps. 80:4

It began as an 8 foot banyan tree transplanted to Lahina, Maui from India, and has stood there for 150 years. A cultural landmark, it dominates the central square in the usual pattern of banyan trees, spreading its branch-supporting pillars that look like new tree trunks. It has about 46 major trunks and is the largest of its kind in the US, more than 60 feet high. Its shade provided a cool resting place for residents and tourists alike. This summer's devastating fire charred its beauty, stripping the tree of its life-giving leaves, leaving it for dead. Because of its unique history and age, volunteers worked to help preserve the banyan tree. Unable and unwilling to give it up, they composted, they watered, they watched carefully. The tree has unofficially become symbolic of the disaster that killed so many and destroyed villages. Slowly but surely, tiny new leaves began to show. The tree survived the devastation and has begun to show new life. It has become a sign of hope for the people of Maui, a sign of new beginnings, the promise of hope for the future. God has not left his people destitute. In the new life of that banyan tree, God reminds his people that he is with them and that he will heal their broken spirits and raise them up again.

Banyan tree on the estate of Henry Ford, Ft. Meyers, FL

"On the first day of Christmas my true love gave to me…." All right, admit it. When you first started reading these words, the song started in your mind. The Twelve Days of Christmas song has become the most tedious of the Christmas carols. Which is too bad because it removes the concept of the twelve beautiful days we call the Christmas Season. There are so many different aspects of the birth of Christ that they can't be captured in just one day. The Church's liturgical calendar breaks open the story of the Nativity into smaller parts so we can have the time to absorb the many lessons of each contributing part. We celebrate the feasts of people who have been a part of our faith: St. John the Evangelist, St. Stephen, the first martyr, the Holy Family, the Holy Innocents, the Wise Men, on through to St. John the Baptist who is the transition point to the ministry of the Man, Jesus. We celebrate the the Holy Family's flight into Egypt, the Child Jesus lost in the Temple. So, Christmas is not just one day. Life shouldn't go back to the old routine on December 26. There are many more days to unwrap our Christmas treasures. We are still celebrating each day when Christ comes into our lives in and through one another. Merry Christmas. Feliz Navidad!

"May the wonders of this season stay with you."

Anon

Christmas creche, Mercy Center, Rochester, NY

"Read it again!" How many times has a parent heard their child demand a certain story book to be read again and again. The child may have heard the story so many times they could recite it by heart, as can the story teller. Yet, "Read it again!" prevails.

The Christian Churches are beginning a new church year. The story of Christ begins to be told again. It begins with the prophecies of Isaiah in our Advent readings and continues to be told through to November of next year. During these many months we hear stories of the man Jesus and of his ministry to the people of Israel. We will hear about the people who were a part of his family tree and about the early Church that grew after him. And, yes, we have read the story before, every year in fact. The details have not changed but our hearing of them has. We have different ears to hear with this year than we had last year. The words may mean something new if we listen with care, if we let them sit in our hearts. This is why we call the Bible the "living Word". We hear differently each time the Words are proclaimed. Let reading the Scriptures again be part of your Advent preparation for the big story of the coming of Christ, the Savior. "Read it again!" and again, and again.

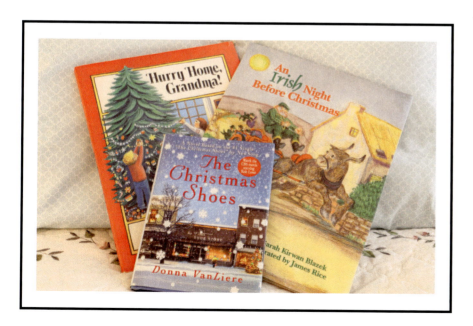

"The Word of the Lord be with you"

Christmas Reading

My flowers did a happy dance in the rain yesterday. So, too, my vegetables. It was a very welcome rain. A "real soaker", as my father would say. It's a small garden, just enough to give my green thumb some exercise. I was reminded of a gardening lesson I learned from my Dad. It had been a dry spell and we needed rain. When we had a sudden thunderstorm, I was excited because now the earth was watered. It was a brief storm but I thought it was enough. But Dad put his finger into the ground and showed the dry dirt that was underneath. The rain only covered the surface and wasn't enough to nourish the roots below. We needed a real soaker, not a passing storm. Sometimes our relationships with others are like the dry, water-starved soil. We are content with just the surface watering we do, thinking that it is enough. We know each other superficially and judge by what we see on the surface without coming to know the depth of a person's heart. Relationships that are shallow don't last but the ones that we work hard to cultivate can be game changers. We need to keep the soil of friendship watered and tended to. We need more than just a passing storm, we need a "real soaker" And who knows what treasures we will find below the surface. Get to know one another. Don't be content to say it is enough. Keep watering the roots of friendship and foster new ones. And we will find great abundance.

"I will send you rain in its season, and the ground will yield its crops and the trees their fruit.

Leviticus 26:4

Summer garden

> *"The art of creation is an act of hope."*
> Anon

Almost perfect! Summer's garden offers this beautiful flower. It is absolutely stunning. While it catches your breath with its glory, you know that its beauty is fleeting. Its time of existence is short. Yet it serves its purpose of being. It gives us the awareness of the Creator who has nourished it into life, a God who delights in what he has created. If God is so delighted with this one little dahlia, how much more so is he delighted with us, the ones he has created in his own image and likeness. We, too, are his vessels of beauty, bringing to others the awareness of God's presence. We do so even though we often show the flaws that our humanness exhibit. But, unlike the dahlia bloom, we have been gifted with the ability to transform that which is flawed into moments of beauty. We are still in the process of becoming that for which we have been created. We are continually invited to be perfect as our heavenly Father is perfect. And that is our lifelong purpose: to be perfect in the eyes of our God. It is this that really matters. How do you radiate God's beauty this day?

The Garden's offering - a lavender dahlia bloom

Credits

Scripture texts in this work are taken from the New American Bible, revised edition © 2010, 1991, 1986, 1970 Confraternity of Christian Doctrine, Washington, D.C. and are used by permission of the copyright owner. All Rights Reserved. No part of the New American Bible may be reproduced in any form without permission in writing from the copyright owner.

The hymn **"For the Beauty of the Earth"** written by Folliott Sandford Pierpoint, 1835-1917, is in the Public Domain.

Many individual quotes have been found in uncopyrighted printed articles with the sources unmentioned.

Photography by Sister Kathleen M. O'Connell, RSM